FIRST STEPS FOR
NEW CHRISTIANS

ESTABLISHING BIBLICAL **DIRECTION** FOR NEW CHRISTIANS

PAUL CHAPPELL

First published in 2008 by Striving Together Publications, a ministry of
Lancaster Baptist Church, Lancaster, CA 93535. Striving Together Publications
is committed to providing tried, trusted, and proven books that will further
equip local churches to carry out the Great Commission. Your comments and
suggestions are valued.

Striving Together Publications
4020 E. Lancaster Blvd.
Lancaster, CA 93535
800.201.7748

Edited by Andrew Jones
Cover design and layout by Andrew Jones
Special thanks to our proofreaders.

We recognize that many of the quotes and illustrations mentioned
in this book are derived from a myriad of sources and are not
original with the author. To preserve the accuracy and authenticity
of each illustration the facts remain unchanged. We do not take credit
for those illustrations whose sources we cannot locate.

ISBN 978-1-59894-063-3

Printed in the United States of America

Table of Contents

INTRODUCTION

Congratulations on your decision to accept Jesus Christ as your personal Lord and Saviour. You will never make a more important decision. When you became a Christian, not only was your eternal destiny settled, but you were also given the opportunity to begin life with a fresh start—a new hope. The Bible says in 2 Corinthians 5:17, *"Therefore if any man be in Christ, he is a new creature: old things are passed away; behold, all things are become new."*

Since you have accepted Christ, you have become a new person in Him! But your growth as a Christian is just beginning. Although the most important decision has been made, there are many things to learn in the days ahead. You see, Christianity is more than mere religion; it is a day by day personal relationship with Jesus Christ.

First Steps for New Christians is designed to help you begin a joyful, fulfilling relationship with the Lord. It covers topics that address the foundational beliefs of Bible-believing Christians. This booklet was written to coincide with God's Word. Each subject begins with a brief introduction, and all of the subjects have key terms and definitions so that you can understand the terminology used by many pastors and churches today.

Each subject has been developed into a study for the purpose of allowing you to better understand the Bible. Our intention is for you to discover what God says about being a Christian. Second Timothy 2:15 states, *"Study to shew thyself approved unto God, a workman that needeth not to be ashamed, rightly dividing the word of truth."* As a new believer, it is important for you to understand your newfound faith in God. In a day when there is so much deception and heartache, you must be able to clearly comprehend the truth.

To get started, get your Bible and a pen. Find a quiet place, and ask the Lord to help you understand these truths. Purpose to look up every verse using the reference guide in the front of your Bible. As you read each verse, fill in the empty blanks.

As you discover these truths and apply them to your life, you will begin to see God bless your life in unbelievable ways. Life can be tough, but when you have the Lord on your side, you will face life refreshed and with new hope. Our prayer is that *First Steps for New Christians* will be a helpful and encouraging resource as you begin your new life in Christ.

Sincerely,

Paul Chappell

Pastor Paul Chappell

CHAPTER ONE

OUR SINFUL CONDITION BEFORE SALVATION

We have all known the difference between right and wrong from a very young age. Even as a child, our obedience was a choice. No one has ever been perfect. In fact, doing those things that displease God is part of our nature.

Disobedience (or sin) began when Adam and Eve ate the forbidden fruit in the garden of Eden. God had created a perfect environment for them, yet He gave them the ability to disobey. He wanted their love to be a free choice. The punishment for their sin was great. Their bodies and souls were corrupted by sin, and they were separated from God—the only source of life. Since that day, the whole world has been affected by Adam's disobedience, and all future generations inherited his sin nature.

ILLUSTRATION

If you find an apple with a worm hole, it does not mean there is a worm inside the apple. It simply means that an insect laid an egg in the apple blossom. Sometime later, the worm hatched in the heart of the apple, then ate its way out. Sin is in the very blossom of our human nature. Like the worm, it begins in the heart and works its way out through our thoughts, words, and actions. What we see coming out is what has been born on the inside.

QUOTE

"Man is not a sinner because he sins. He sins because he is a sinner."—**Source Unknown**

Man has a problem, and it is on the inside. Evolution teaches that man is a sinner because he has not fully developed. The educator says that there is no such thing as "sin;" it is only ignorance. If we can give better education, then we could do away with sin. But the Bible teaches in Ephesians 2:3 that we are *"by nature the children of wrath."* That is why *reformation* can never replace *repentance*. A man may try to improve his life by reforming his appearance, but in his heart he would still be a sinner.

ILLUSTRATION

A lumberjack can take a crooked tree out of the forest, bring it to the sawmill, and trim off all four sides of the tree to create a perfectly straight and even board. But if you were to stand that board up and look at it from the end, the heart of that wood would still be crooked.

That is what reformation is. No matter how much a man endeavors to straighten his life, the Bible still refers to his heart in Jeremiah 17:9 as being *"deceitful above all things, and desperately wicked."*

« IMPORTANT TERMS

» **Sin:** anything that is offensive or contrary to God's laws

» **Soul:** the spiritual part of our being that continues after death, also referred to as our spirit

» **Hell:** the eternal dwelling place of those who reject Christ

» **Heaven:** the dwelling place of God and the home of believers after physical death

 « KEY BIBLE TRUTHS

What was our condition before Christ saved us?

We were spiritually blind.

Our spiritual understanding was marred by sin. Satan had shrouded us from the light of the Gospel.

"In whom the god of this world hath _____ the minds of them which believe not, lest the _____ of the glorious _____ of Christ, who is the image of God, should shine unto them."—2 Corinthians 4:4

We were lost in sin.

Jesus Christ came to seek us as lost children and to draw us back to our loving, Heavenly Father.

"For the _____ of man is come to _____ and to save that which was _____."—Luke 19:10

We were separated from Christ.

Before we accepted Christ as our Saviour, our sin separated us from God. Only Jesus Christ could bridge the span that isolated us from the Heavenly Father.

"Having the understanding darkened, being _____

from the life of God through the _____ that is in

them, because of the _____ of their heart:"

—EPHESIANS 4:18

We were guilty before a just God.

When we commit a crime or break the law, there is a punishment for our wrongdoing. We call this justice. God is also just, and when we disobey His laws, we face the consequences for our disobedience.

"He that _____ on the Son hath

_____ life: and he that believeth not the _____

shall not see _____; but the _____ of

God abideth on him."—JOHN 3:36

We were spiritually dead in our sins.

Our sin separated us from God and from everlasting life in Heaven. Once we accepted Jesus Christ as our Saviour, we were no longer facing an eternity in Hell. We became alive in Christ.

 ILLUSTRATION

If you were relating to someone that your car had stalled at an intersection that morning, you would say, "My car died this morning." What you mean is—it stopped. When the

Bible speaks of being "dead" it is not in reference to *stoppage* but rather *separation.*

"And _____ hath he quickened, who were _____ in

_____ and _____:"—EPHESIANS 2:1

We were servants of sin.

Before Jesus Christ freed us through the shedding of His blood on the Cross, we were in spiritual bondage and held captive by our sins.

"But _____ be thanked, that ye were the _____ of sin,

but ye have _____ from the _____ that form of

_____ which was delivered you."—ROMANS 6:17

We were headed for the Lake of Fire.

Because God is holy, He cannot allow sin into Heaven. Therefore, those who reject Christ will be separated from God for all of eternity.

"And whosoever was not found written in the

_____ ____ _____ was cast into the _____

____ _____."—REVELATION 20:15

💡 ILLUSTRATION

A forest fire was ravaging a rural community. Firefighters were quickly dispatched to the scene to extinguish the fiery inferno. After hours of battling the fire, some men were surrounded by flames. An airplane flew over and dropped weighted notes warning them, "You are surrounded and will perish unless you take action immediately. There is one narrow corridor of escape, and before long it will be cut off."

They received a message from above telling them something they could not have known amidst the smoke and furor. Thankfully, they did not question the authenticity or the reliability of the notes but acted on them and were saved.

We live in a culture surrounded by a barrage of "alternative ways" to Heaven, and God is saying, "There is only one way of escape, and it is through My Son." Jesus said in John 14:6, "…*I am the way, the truth, and the life: no man cometh unto the Father, but by me.*" The only chance an unsaved man has of escaping the eternal fires of Hell is through accepting the narrow message of salvation. "*Enter ye in at the strait gate: for wide is the gate, and broad is the way, that leadeth to destruction, and many there be which go in thereat*" (Matthew 7:13).

CHAPTER TWO

UNDERSTANDING GOD'S SALVATION

Because we are born sinners, we are already condemned and under God's judgment. If we refuse the Son of God, Jesus Christ, our punishment as sinners is Hell. Our religious works, offerings, church attendance, baptism, or any other good deeds cannot change our sinful condition before God.

God displayed His love by sending His Son, Jesus Christ, to die on the Cross for our sins. Because of Christ, we can come to God by faith. We can do nothing to earn salvation; it is the gift of God. We must believe that Jesus Christ is risen from the dead, and ask Him to forgive and save us by trusting in Him alone as the final payment for our sin.

« IMPORTANT TERMS

» **Salvation:** the "saving" of a sinner from the judgment of sin

» **Condemned:** declared guilty as sinners before God

» **Forgiveness:** the pardon or remission of an offense or crime

» **Atonement:** the removal of sin or uncleanness by the blood of Jesus Christ

» **Justification:** an act of free grace by which God pardons the sinner and accepts him as righteous (holy, good) on account of the atonement of Christ

» **Propitiation:** satisfaction or appeasment, specifically towards God

 « KEY BIBLE TRUTHS

We must realize that God loves us.

God showed His love to the whole world by sending His only Son, Jesus Christ, to die on the Cross for our sins.

"For God so _____ the world, that he _____ his only begotten _____, that whosoever believeth in him should not _____, but have _____ _____."

—JOHN 3:16

"Herein is love, not that we loved God, but that he loved us,

and sent his Son to be the _____ for our sins."

—1 JOHN 4:10

We must understand that all of us have sinned.

Sin is anything that displeases God (lying, stealing, disobedience, unkindness, etc.). Although we may feel that we are not wicked people, we are still sinners. It is always sin that separates man from God.

"For all have _____, and come _____ of the

glory of God;"—ROMANS 3:23

💡 **ILLUSTRATION**

There were many who sailed on board the *Titanic*—some who traveled with very fine accommodations, and others who rode below in the steerage. But when the final tally came back to the New York office they put them in only two categories—saved and lost. Some people may unwittingly be going to Hell first class—thinking they are too good to be punished. But in God's eyes, we are all equally sinful.

💬 **QUOTE**

"The worst form of badness is human goodness."
—Source Unknown

"But we are all as an unclean thing, and all our

righteousnesses are as filthy _____; and we all do fade

as a leaf; and our _____, like the wind, have

taken us away."—ISAIAH 64:6

We must recognize that death is the punishment for our sin.
When we break a law, the government requires a punishment or a payment for our disobedience. It does not matter whether we violate a traffic law or whether we commit murder, there is still a punishment. When we disobey God, we fall short of His glory, and are destined to eternal separation in Hell.

"He that believeth on him is not condemned: but he that

believeth not is condemned _____, because he hath

not believed in the name of the only begotten Son of God."

—JOHN 3:18

💡 ILLUSTRATION

If a dog has rabies, it is destroyed. The dog may not have even bitten a victim, yet it is still killed. Not because of what the dog has done, but because of what the dog is capable of doing. It is not just the sins we commit that destine us for punishment; it is also our sinful nature that condemns us.

"For the wages of sin is _____; but the _____ of

God is eternal life through _____ _____ our

Lord."—ROMANS 6:23

💬 QUOTE

Salvation is not a reward for the righteous; it is a gift for the guilty. Salvation is not a goal to be achieved; it is a gift to be received.

"For by grace are ye saved through _____; and that

not of yourselves: it is the _____ of God: Not of works,

lest any man should boast."—EPHESIANS 2:8–9

We must realize that Jesus Christ died to pay our price.

Before we were even born, God knew that we would be sinners and unable to get to Heaven on our own account. Therefore, He sent His Son to pay our sin penalty by shedding His blood on the Cross.

"But God commendeth his _____ toward us, in that, while we were yet sinners, Christ _____ for us."

—ROMANS 5:8

We must believe on Jesus Christ, and claim His promise of eternal life.

The only righteousness that God will accept is sinless perfection. And that was accomplished through His Son Jesus Christ. Romans 3:22 says, *"Even the righteousness of God which is by faith of Jesus Christ unto all and upon all them that believe...."* Romans 10:10 says, *"For with the heart man believeth unto righteousness; and with the mouth confession is made unto salvation."*

Do you know what it means to believe and confess that Jesus is Lord? It literally means that you agree with God.

There are only two ways to be saved: If you live a sinless life (which no one has done, except Jesus) or you ask Jesus to take the payment of your sin for you (which He did on the Cross), and accept His righteousness on your behalf. Second Corinthians 5:21 says, *"For he hath made him to be sin for us, who knew no sin; that we might be made the righteousness of God in him."*

God's requirements are simple. He asks us to believe on Jesus Christ and to call upon Him for salvation.

*"For whosoever shall _____ upon the _____ of
the Lord shall be _____."*—ROMANS 10:13

*"That if thou shalt _____ with thy mouth the Lord
Jesus, and shalt _____ in thine heart that God
hath raised him from dead, thou shalt be _____. For
with the heart man believeth unto righteousness; and with
the mouth confession is made unto salvation."*
—ROMANS 10:9–10

 **ILLUSTRATION**

In 1829, George Wilson was sentenced to be hanged in the
state of Pennsylvania for murder. For whatever reason,
President Andrew Jackson pardoned Wilson.

When the pardon was presented to Wilson, he refused
it. As a result, Wilson was hung by the neck until dead, even
though a pardon had been offered.

God offers a pardon to anyone who places their faith in
His only Son—Jesus. But the pardon is no good if refused.
Isaiah 55:7 promises, *"Let the wicked forsake his way, and the
unrighteous man his thoughts: and let him return unto the
LORD, and he will have mercy upon him; and to our God, for
he will abundantly **pardon**."*

CHAPTER THREE

OUR NEW LIFE IN CHRIST

Jesus is in the transformation business. He is transforming people like me and like you. Someone wisely said, "Nature forms us, sin deforms us, education informs us, penitentiaries reform us, but Jesus transforms us."

There is only one person who has ever lived the perfect Christian life. It is not you, and it is not me. It is Jesus.

Why? Because what Jesus began to do in His life on earth, He wants to continue to do through every child of God. Jesus Christ wants to live His life through you. The Apostle Paul said, *"To whom God would make known what is the riches of the glory of this mystery among the Gentiles; **which is Christ in you**, the hope of glory"* (Colossians 1:27).

What a wonderful thing it is to know that we have hope in Jesus Christ and an eternal home in Heaven! God no longer sees us as sinners, but as dear children. Once we have accepted Him as our Saviour, we are born again into the family of God.

Although there will still be times when we displease Him or break His laws, God, as our loving Heavenly Father, seeks to restore fellowship and draw us closer to Him.

 ## « IMPORTANT TERMS

» **Holy Spirit (Holy Ghost):** the third person of the Godhead (God the Father, Jesus the Son, and the Holy Spirit)

» **Born again:** new birth into the family of God occurs when one accepts Christ

» **Saved:** refers to one who has accepted God's gift of salvation

 ## « KEY BIBLE TRUTHS

We become children of God.

By simply receiving Christ as our Saviour, God empowers us to become His children. We then enter into a new and permanent relationship as part of God's family.

"But as many as _____ him, to them gave he _____ to become the _____ of God, even to them that _____ on his _____:"—JOHN 1:12

"Behold, what manner of love the Father hath bestowed upon us, that we should be called the _____ of God: therefore the world knoweth us not, because it knew him not."—1 JOHN 3:1

The Holy Ghost dwells in us permanently.

After we receive Christ, the Holy Ghost (Holy Spirit) comes to dwell inside of us. He has purchased us for His possession; our bodies become His temple (dwelling place).

"What? Know ye not that your body is the _____ of the

_____ _____ which is in you, which ye have of

_____, and ye are not your own?"—1 CORINTHIANS 6:19

The day we were saved God placed the righteousness of Jesus Christ on our account. Those who are saved have been declared righteous.

 ILLUSTRATION

There was a Christian maid named Betty who worked for a ruthless infidel. He constantly ridiculed her faith in God.

One day he asked her in a cynical voice, "Betty what does it feel like to be saved?"

Betty said, "I don't know if I could fully explain it to where you could understand, but it feels to me like I'm standing in Jesus' shoes, and He is standing in mine."

A theologian could not have said it better. God took our sin, and we took His righteousness. Second Corinthians 5:21 says, *"For he hath made him to be sin for us, who knew no sin; that we might be made the righteousness of God in him."*

We become new creatures.

We are changed the day we accept Christ—we receive a new nature. This does not mean that we will never be tempted to do wrong things; rather, we now have the Lord to help us live lives that please Him.

"Therefore if any man be in _____, he is a new _____: old things are passed away; behold, all things are become _____."—2 Corinthians 5:17

ILLUSTRATION

Years ago, a young missionary wife moved to another country with her husband. She looked at the dirty floor in their new house, promptly grabbed a brush and pail, and got down on her hands and knees and began to scrub.

She scrubbed and scrubbed and mopped and rinsed and scrubbed and scrubbed and mopped and rinsed, but she could not get the dirt off the floor. One of the locals revealed the reason for her problem by telling her, "The reason you can't get the dirt off the floor is because it's a dirt floor!"

Some people try to live the same way. They endeavor to clean up their life hoping they will be more acceptable to God. But it is only after salvation that the old man becomes a new man in Jesus Christ.

"Being confident of this very thing, that he which hath begun a good _____ in you will perform it until the day of Jesus Christ:"—Philippians 1:6

The Holy Spirit seals us.

God sends His Holy Spirit to seal every believer. The Spirit is our promise that we have eternal life through Jesus Christ.

"In whom ye also _____, after that ye heard the word of _____, the _____ of your _____: in whom also after that ye _____, ye were _____ with that _____ _____ of promise, Which is the

earnest of our inheritance until the _____ *of*
the _____ *possession, unto the* _____ *of his*
glory."—EPHESIANS 1:13–14

What happens after we have received Christ?

1. God becomes our Father; we become His children (1 John 3:2).
2. Because we are family, God deals with us as sons, not as sinners.
3. We can do nothing to break this relationship. God will not disown His children. Sometimes our *fellowship* may be strained, but the *relationship* remains the same.
4. Our Father will never do anything to hurt us purposely (Matthew 7:11).
5. We will be protected (Matthew 18:6).
6. We will be cared for (Philippians 4:19).
7. We will be corrected and taught (Hebrews 12:5–11).

CHAPTER FOUR

ETERNAL SECURITY

By accepting the Lord Jesus Christ as our Saviour, we are saved now and forever! We have God's promises, which are found in His Word. The Spirit of God lives within us, and our new relationship to God gives us the assurance of eternal life in Heaven.

There may be times when we wonder if we are truly saved. When doubts come into our hearts, we must remember that whether or not we feel saved, the Bible promises that *"…whosoever believeth in him should not perish, but have everlasting life"* (John 3:16).

 ILLUSTRATION

During initial construction on the Golden Gate Bridge, no safety devices were used and twenty-three men fell to their deaths. For the final part of the project, however, a large net was used as a safety precaution. At least ten men fell into it and were saved from certain death. Even more interesting, however, is the fact that twenty-five percent more work was accomplished after the net was installed. Why? Because the men had the assurance of their safety, and they were free to wholeheartedly serve the project.

When a Christian has the hope of eternal life, and the assurance that never again will he come under condemnation, his potential for Christ is unlimited.

 « IMPORTANT TERMS

» **Condemnation:** God's judgment

» **Eternal life:** everlasting life in God's presence

» **Righteousness:** an attribute of holiness that belongs to God alone

» **Redemption:** Christ paid the price for our sins and freed us from bondage

» **Book of Life:** a book kept by God that lists the names of those who have accepted Christ

 « KEY BIBLE TRUTHS

We have everlasting life in Heaven.

The moment we receive Christ as our Saviour, our eternal destiny is settled. We no longer have to worry about life after death; we have the promise of eternity in Heaven with God. Everlasting life is not something you get when you die. Everlasting life is something you get when you receive Jesus. If I have everlasting life, when can it end? Suppose I had it ten years and it ended. Did I have everlasting life? No, I had a ten-year life. Whatever you have, if it can be lost, then it was not everlasting.

"Verily, verily, I say unto you, He that _____ my word, and _____ on him that sent me, hath _____ life, and shall not come into _____; but is passed from death unto life."—JOHN 5:24

We are kept by the power of God.

There are many possessions in life that will one day fade away—but not salvation. The Bible promises that we are kept by the power of God.

"Blessed be the God and Father of our Lord Jesus Christ, which according to his abundant mercy hath begotten us again unto a lively hope by the resurrection of Jesus Christ from the dead, To an inheritance incorruptible, and undefiled, and that fadeth not away, _____ in heaven for you, Who are _____ by the power of God through faith unto salvation ready to be revealed in the last time."
—1 PETER 1:3–5

We are in the grip of God's grace.

As Christians, there is nothing we can ever do or say that will cause us to fall out of favor with God. We are held by His mighty grip.

QUOTE

If I did nothing to earn salvation, I can do nothing to lose it.

"And I give unto them eternal life; and they shall never perish,

neither shall any man _____ *them out of my hand."*

—JOHN 10:28

ILLUSTRATION

F.B. Meyer wrote about two Germans who wanted to climb the Matterhorn. They hired three guides and began their ascent at the steepest and most slippery part. The men roped themselves together in this order: guide, traveler, guide, traveler, guide.

They had gone only a little way up the side when the last man lost his footing. He was held up temporarily by the other four, because each had a toehold in the niches they had cut in the ice. But then the next man slipped, and he pulled down the two above him. The only one to stand firm was the first guide, who had driven a spike deep into the ice. Because he held his ground, all the men beneath him regained their footing.

F.B. Meyer concluded his story by drawing a spiritual application. He said, "I am like one of those men who slipped, but thank God, I am bound in a living partnership to Christ. And because He stands, I will never perish."

God will never cast us out of His family.

When we accept Christ, we are born again into the family of God. Once we become a child of God, we remain His child for all of eternity. There is nothing we can do to cause God to disown us.

"All that the _____ giveth me shall come to me; and him

that cometh to me I will in no wise _____ out."—JOHN 6:37

We have the gift of eternal life.

A gift is free—it is not something one earns, and once it has been received, it cannot be taken back. Salvation is God's gift to us that we possess for all of eternity.

"…but the _____ of God is _____ life through _____

_____ our Lord."—ROMANS 6:23B

Anyone who calls upon the name of the Lord shall be saved.

God promises us that anyone can ask Jesus Christ for eternal life in Heaven. His gift is not limited to a race, to the rich, to the poor, etc. Salvation is offered to all who believe in Jesus Christ and ask Him to be their personal Saviour.

"For _____ shall _____ upon the name of the

_____ shall be _____."—ROMANS 10:13

We have been made the righteousness of God.

Jesus Christ, the perfect Son of God, became sin for us so that we could be justified (declared righteous) before God.

"For he hath made him to be _____ for us, who knew no

sin; that we might be made the _____ of

_____ in him."—2 CORINTHIANS 5:21

Christ dwells in our hearts by faith.

The primary idea of faith is trust. When we make the decision by faith (trust) to accept Jesus Christ, He comes to dwell in our hearts.

"That _____ may dwell in your _____ by faith..."—Ephesians 3:17a

We have redemption through Christ's blood.

Redemption means "to free someone from bondage." For redemption to be possible, a price must be paid. Jesus Christ paid the price for redemption with His blood.

"In whom we have _____ through his blood, even the _____ of sins:"—Colossians 1:14

Christ washed our sins away.

Jesus Christ shed His blood on the Cross to wash our sins away so that our hearts could be cleansed and made new.

"And from Jesus Christ, who is the faithful witness, and the first begotten of the dead, and the prince of the kings of the earth. Unto him that loved us, and _____ us from our sins in his own blood."—Revelation 1:5

Our names are written in the Lamb's Book of Life.

When we accepted Christ as our Saviour our names were written in the Lamb's Book of Life. Those whose names are not recorded will be cast into Hell.

"And there shall in no wise enter into it any thing that defileth, neither whatsoever worketh abomination, or maketh a lie: but they which are _____ in the Lamb's book of life."—REVELATION 21:27

Nothing can separate you from the love of God.

Neither death nor anything that happens after death, or anything that happens while you are living can separate you from God's love.

"For I am persuaded, that neither death, nor life, nor angels, nor principalities, nor powers, nor things present, nor things to come, Nor height, nor depth, nor any other creature, shall be able to _____ us from the love of God, which is in Christ Jesus our Lord."—ROMANS 8:38–39

We are in Christ.

You are in Christ just as Noah was in the ark. The ark was a picture of Jesus. When Noah went into the ark, God shut the door. Noah may have fallen down a lot of times in that ark, but he never fell out of it. Your security is not in a place; it is in a Person, and His name is Jesus.

"Therefore if any man be _____ Christ, he is a new creature: old things are passed away; behold, all things are become new."—2 CORINTHIANS 5:17

We are sealed by the Holy Spirit of promise.

God places His seal on the life of every believer—a promise that can never be broken.

"And grieve not the holy Spirit of God, whereby ye are

_____ *unto the day of redemption."*

—EPHESIANS 4:30

The Lord Jesus Christ is ever interceding for you.

Jesus said in John 17:9, *"I pray for them: I pray not for the world, but for them which thou hast given me; for they are thine."* Jesus also prayed, *"I pray not that thou shouldest take them out of the world, but that thou shouldest keep them from the evil…Neither pray I for these alone, but for them also which shall believe on me through their word"* (John 17:15, 20).

Say your name in that verse because Jesus prayed for you! Has Jesus ever prayed a prayer that was not answered? Of course, the answer is "No."

"And I knew that thou hearest me _____: *but because of the people which stand by I said it, that they may believe that thou hast sent me."*—JOHN 11:42

"Wherefore he is able also to save them to the _____ *that come unto God by him, seeing he ever liveth to make* _____ *for them."*—HEBREWS 7:25

CHAPTER FIVE

BAPTISM: THE FIRST STEP OF OBEDIENCE

While baptism is not required for salvation, it is an important step of obedience to Christ. By following the Lord in believer's baptism, we are obeying Christ and showing Him that we are glad He is our Saviour. We experience the blessing of committing ourselves to Christ through our public identification with Him.

The Christian who refuses to be baptized could be compared to a wife who refuses to accept her wedding ring. How can our relationship with Christ start off right if we refuse to follow Him, and if we are ashamed of Him before others?

Baptism is not something to fear. If you have accepted Christ and want to follow Him in baptism, simply step forward during the invitation of the next church service. Someone will be happy to help you. Let them know that you would like to follow the Lord in believer's baptism. Choose to make this important first step in your Christian life soon. You won't regret it!

« IMPORTANT TERMS

>> **Immersion:** to completely cover in water
>> **Resurrection:** raised from the dead

 ## « KEY BIBLE TRUTHS

What is baptism?

The Bible teaches that baptism is a symbol—an outward expression of an inward decision. In the life of every Christian, it is an important step of obedience to God that signifies our faith in Christ. As a wedding ring identifies a husband with his wife, so baptism identifies a Christian with Christ.

"Know ye not, that so many of us as were _____ into

_____ _____ were baptized into his _____?

Therefore we are _____ with him by _____

into death: that like as _____ was raised up from the

dead by the _____ of the Father, even so we also should

_____ in newness of life. For if we have been planted

together in the _____ of his death, we shall be also in

the likeness of his _____:"—ROMANS 6:3–5

Is baptism for me?

The Bible teaches that baptism is for anyone who has personally accepted Jesus Christ as Saviour. Baptism does not save us or wash away our sins. It is simply an outward expression of an inward decision to accept Christ. If you have accepted Christ and have never been baptized, you should choose to be baptized as soon as possible.

"…and the eunuch said, See, here is water; what doth hinder me to be baptized? And Philip said, If thou believest with all thine _____, thou mayest. And he answered and said, I believe that Jesus Christ is the _____ of God. And he commanded the chariot to stand still: and they went down both into the _____, both Philip and the eunuch; and he _____ him."—Acts 8:36b–38

Why should I be baptized?

There are three biblical reasons to be baptized:

1. Christ commands it.

   "Go ye therefore, and teach all nations, _____ them in the name of the Father, and of the Son, and of the Holy Ghost:"—Matthew 28:19

2. Christ was our example.

   "Then cometh Jesus from Galilee to Jordan unto John, to be _____ of him."—Matthew 3:13

3. Believers in the Bible practiced baptism.

   "Then they gladly _____ his word and were baptized…"—Acts 2:41a

How should I be baptized?

The word *baptize* literally means "to plunge or to dunk."
The Bible teaches that you should be baptized in water by
immersion rather than sprinkling. Only immersion correctly
pictures baptism as Christ's death, burial, and resurrection.

"John answered them, saying, I baptize with _____..."
—JOHN 1:26A

"And it came to pass in those days, that Jesus came from
Nazareth of Galilee, and was _____ of John in
Jordan. And straightway coming up out of the _____,
he saw the heavens opened, and the Spirit like a dove
descending upon him:"—MARK 1:9–10

"And he commanded the chariot to stand still: and they went
down both _____ the water, both Philip and the eunuch;
and he _____ him."—ACTS 8:38

picturing Christ's death   His burial   and His resurrection

When should I be baptized?

In the Bible, baptism always took place right after salvation.
Rather than taking a thirteen-week course before you can
be baptized, you should choose to be baptized as soon as
you can after your salvation decision.

"And brought them out, and said, Sirs, what must I do to be saved? And they said, _____ on the Lord Jesus Christ, and thou shalt be _____, and thy house. And they spake unto him the word of the Lord, and to all that were in his house. And he took them the same hour of the night, and washed their stripes; and was _____, he and all his, _____."—ACTS 16:30–33*

"Then they that gladly received his _____ were baptized: and the same _____ there were _____ unto them about three thousand souls."—ACTS 2:41*

QUOTE
"Nothing is more plainly taught in the New Testament than that it is the duty of every believer in Christ to be baptized."
—Charles Spurgeon

CHAPTER SIX

THE LOCAL CHURCH

Once you have accepted Christ as your Saviour, it is important to attend a Bible-believing church. Ephesians 5:25 says that *"…Christ also loved the church, and gave himself for it."* Although church attendance does not save us or get us to Heaven, it is very important to God and is a vital aspect of Christian growth.

The Bible-believing church is more than a building; it is a place where Christians meet together to grow in God's Word, to glorify God, and to build lasting friendships with people who want to know God more. Hebrews 10:25 says, *"Not forsaking the assembling of ourselves together, as the manner of some is; but exhorting one another: and so much the more, as ye see the day approaching."* Dr. Lee Roberson, a renowned preacher for over seventy years, referred to church attendance as "Three to thrive: Sunday morning, Sunday evening, and Wednesday evening."

« IMPORTANT TERMS

» **Preach:** to proclaim the Word of God

» **Fellowship:** a gathering of Christians who share the same bond in Christ; friendship with fellow believers

» **Worship:** giving God the honor, glory, and praise that He deserves

 « KEY BIBLE TRUTHS

What is the purpose of the local church?

To preach the Word of God

At church, we listen to the pastor proclaim the truths of God's Word. Bible preaching works in our hearts and helps us grow into spiritual maturity.

"And when they were at Salamis, they _____ the word of God in the _____ of the Jews: and they had also John to their _____."—Acts 13:5

To provide fellowship

Church provides us a place where we can meet people who desire to serve the Lord and live for Him. Christian friends are vital in helping us grow spiritually.

"And they _____ stedfastly in the apostles' doctrine and _____, and in breaking of bread, and in _____."—Acts 2:42

To provide oversight

God has given you a gift—a pastor—a loving under-shepherd to encourage, edify, and equip your life for spiritual growth and fruitfulness. There is no doubt that the devil fights this relationship! After all, this is the man who will teach and preach the Word of God to your family. This is one of the few who will weep with you when you hurt, encourage you when you fail, seek you when you wander, and pray for you throughout your Christian journey. A wise Christian will establish a strong relationship with his pastor.

"Obey them that have the rule over you, and submit yourselves: for they _____ for your souls, as they that must give account, that they may do it with joy, and not with grief: for that is unprofitable for you."—HEBREWS 13:17

To practice baptism

The Bible tells us that baptism is to be practiced in the local church. Baptism not only shows that we have believed on Christ, it also identifies us with that local body of believers.

"And Crispus, the chief ruler of the synagogue, _____ on the Lord with all his house; and many of the Corinthians hearing believed, and were _____."—ACTS 18:8

To observe the Lord's Supper

An ordinance is the outward sign of an inward work. Jesus only established two ordinances for us to observe—baptism and the Lord's Supper. The Lord's Supper is also referred to as the Lord's Table or Communion, which speaks of the relationship between Jesus and believers. The Lord's Table was instituted by Christ specifically as a way for the local church to reflect upon the suffering and death of Christ, and to look forward to the prophecy of His Second Coming. It is not a sacrament (something that conveys saving grace).

"For I have received of the Lord that which also I delivered unto you, That the Lord Jesus the same night in which he was betrayed took _____: And when he had given thanks, he brake it, and said, Take, eat: this is my body, which is broken for you: this do in remembrance of me. After the same manner also he took the _____, when he had supped, saying, This cup is the new testament in my blood: this do ye, as oft as ye drink it, in _____ of me. For as often as ye eat this bread, and drink this cup, ye do shew the _____ death till he come. Wherefore whosoever shall eat this bread, and drink this cup of the Lord, unworthily, shall be guilty of the body and blood of the Lord."

—1 Corinthians 11:23–27

To spread the Gospel

God gave the local church the command to reach the lost through telling others, giving, and through supporting world missions. We are called to serve. God has given us a commission. The Apostle Paul said in 2 Corinthians 5:20 *"we are ambassadors for Christ."* The famous songwriter expressed it well when she said that we are to…

> Rescue the perishing, care for the dying,
> Snatch them in pity from sin and the grave;

Weep over the erring one, lift up the fallen,
Tell them of Jesus, the mighty to save.
—**Fanny J. Crosby**

"For _____ shall call upon the name of the Lord
shall be _____. How then shall they call on him in
whom they have not believed? and how shall they _____
in him of whom they have not _____? and how shall
they hear without a _____? And how shall they
_____, except they be sent? as it is written, How
_____ are the feet of them that preach the
_____ of peace, and bring glad tidings of good
things!"—ROMANS 10:13–15

To help God's children grow in grace

Sometimes we will still struggle with doing things that
displease God. The church is a place where we can find
spiritual renewal and restoration.

"Brethren, if a man be overtaken in a _____, ye which
are spiritual, _____ such an one in the spirit of
_____; considering thyself, lest thou also be
tempted."—GALATIANS 6:1

To bring glory to God

God deserves our glory, honor, and praise. It pleases Him
when Christians gather together to worship Him.

"Unto him be _____ in the _____ by Christ Jesus throughout _____ ages, world without end. Amen."
—EPHESIANS 3:21

To restore sinful members

One of our primary responsibilities as a Christian is to care enough about our brothers and sisters in Christ to reach out to them in Christ-like love to help restore them when they have fallen into sin.

"Brethren, if a man be overtaken in a fault, ye which are spiritual, _____ such an one in the spirit of meekness; considering thyself, lest thou also be tempted."
—GALATIANS 6:1

To disciple new believers

Through the services and Sunday school classes of the church, Christians are taught how to live for Christ and serve Him on a day-to-day basis.

"And he gave some, _____; and some, prophets; and some, evangelists; and some, pastors and teachers; For the perfecting of the saints, for the _____ of the ministry, for the _____ of the body of Christ:"—EPHESIANS 4:11–12

To mature new Christians

Christian growth doesn't stop after we accept Christ as our Saviour. It is actually just beginning. At church, we learn how to grow to be more like our Saviour.

"But speaking the _____ in love, may grow up into him
in all things, which is the head, even _____:"
—EPHESIANS 4:15

QUOTE
"Church attendance is as vital to a disciple as a transfusion of rich, healthy blood is to a sick man."—**Dwight L. Moody**

CHAPTER SEVEN

THE BIBLE

God's Word is divided into two sections—the Old and the New Testaments. Even though it is made up of sixty-six books, it has one message. (The sixty-six books are listed in the front of your Bible.) These books are not arranged in chronological order; they are arranged in categories—History, Poetry, Prophets, Gospels, Epistles, and Revelation.

The Bible is a guidebook to Christian living. It contains everything we need to know about our present, our past, and our future. Therefore, as believers we should make regular Bible study a part of our daily activities.

God's favorite name for the Bible is the *Word of God*. More than 3,800 times the Old Testament uses language such as, "Thus saith the Lord" and "The word of the Lord came," claiming divine origin for what is written.

« IMPORTANT TERMS

» **Wisdom:** godly discernment that comes from a knowledge of God's Word

» **Inspiration:** God literally breathed or relayed His words to the human writers

» **Inerrancy:** the Bible is without error

» **Righteousness:** moral purity

» **Doctrine:** what is right according to the Bible

» **Reproof:** what is wrong or displeasing to God

» **Correction:** how to make our wrongs right

» **Instruction in righteousness:** how to stay right

 « KEY BIBLE TRUTHS

Who is the author of the Bible?

The Bible is the Word of God.

Over a period of 1,500 years, God used more than forty different men from a variety of backgrounds to record each word. Most of the human writers God used to pen His words never knew each other; yet, the Bible completely agrees in its entirety and has been proven to be one hundred percent true historically and prophetically.

 ILLUSTRATION

"Take ten contemporary authors and ask them to write their viewpoints on one controversial subject. Would they all agree? No, there would be disagreements between one author and another. Now look at the authorship of the

Bible. All these authors, from a span of 1,500 years, wrote on many controversial subjects, and they do not contradict one another."[1]

"Knowing this first, that no _____ of the scripture is of any private interpretation. For the prophecy came not in old time by the _____ of man: but holy men of God spake as they were _____ by the Holy Ghost."

—2 PETER 1:20–21

1. The Bible was not made by men—*"came not...by the will of man."*
2. Men of God recorded the Bible—*"holy men of God spake..."*
3. God is the author of the Bible—*"moved by the Holy Ghost..."*

"All scripture is given by inspiration of _____, and is profitable for _____, for _____, for correction, for instruction in _____:"—2 TIMOTHY 3:16

QUOTE

"Men do not reject the Bible because it contradicts itself, but because it contradicts them."—**Source Unknown**

How can we defend our Bible?

There are many proofs that support the Bible.

There are many books today that claim to be the Word of God. Many intelligent scholars have written books that attempt to discredit the authority of the Bible. One of Satan's goals is to get man to doubt the Word of God. He did this as early in history as the Garden of Eden. His first words to Eve in Genesis 3:1b were in the form of a question, *"Yea, hath God said, Ye shall not eat of every tree of the garden?"*

The world is in rebellion against God, and worldly people under the influence of Satan seek to destroy your faith. To counter this attack, it is important for Christians to have an answer that will enable them to make a solid defense of their faith when attacked. In the light of the times we live in, it is important for Christians not only to know *what* they believe but also, *why* they believe what they believe.

"But sanctify the Lord God in your hearts: and be ready always to give an _____ to every man that asketh you a reason of the hope that is in you with meekness and fear:"—1 Peter 3:15

"Proving" the trustworthiness of the Bible should be no different than proving any book's reliability. The Bible is reliable not only in matters of "faith and practice" but also in areas of science, history, archaeology, and geography. Here are a few proofs that support the claims of the Bible:

Proof 1: Indestructibility

No other book has been attacked more than the Bible. It has undergone every kind of scrutiny possible from archaeology, science, philosophy, and computers. Yet, despite all these attacks, the Bible proves itself to be true. Each time the skeptics have been wrong, and the Bible has proven itself true.

ILLUSTRATION

Atheist Robert Ingersoll once boasted, "Within fifteen years I'll have the Bible lodged in a morgue." However, within fifteen years of his statement, Robert Ingersoll was lodged within a morgue, and the Bible still lives!

In the eighteenth century the atheist French philosopher Voltaire predicted that within one hundred years, the Bible and Christianity would be swept out of existence and pass into history. Yet just fifty years after his death in 1778, the Geneva Bible Society purchased Voltaire's house and press and began using it as a publishing house for Bibles.

Proof 2: Evidence from Prophecy

Unique among all books ever written, the Bible accurately foretells specific events—in detail—many years, sometimes centuries, before they occur.

 ILLUSTRATION

In approximately 700 BC the prophet Micah named the tiny village of Bethlehem as the birthplace of Israel's Messiah, *"But thou, Bethlehem Ephratah, though thou be little among the thousands of Judah, yet out of thee shall he come forth unto me that is to be ruler in Israel; whose goings forth have been from of old, from everlasting"* (Micah 5:2). The fulfillment of this prophecy in the birth of Christ is one of the most widely known and widely celebrated facts in history.

Proof 3: Evidence from Archaeology

Middle Eastern archaeological investigations have proven the Bible to be true and unerringly accurate in its historical descriptions. Nelson Glueck, a renowned Jewish archaeologist, states, "No archaeological discovery has ever controverted a biblical reference."[2]

Dr. William Albright (1891–1971), the greatest archaeologist of his generation, said this about the Bible: "There can be no doubt that archaeology has confirmed the substantial historicity of the Old Testament."[3]

ILLUSTRATION

For years skeptics thought the story of the falling walls of Jericho was a myth. However, in the 1930s, Dr. John Garstang made a remarkable discovery. He states, "As to the main fact, then, there remains no doubt: the walls fell *outwards* so completely, the attackers would be able to clamber up and over the ruins of the city." This is remarkable because city walls fall *inward*, not *outward*.[4]

Proof 4: Evidence from Science

As communications technology allows information to spread faster, mankind is continually revising scientific theories to match new discoveries. The Bible rises above science by stating facts that have only recently been discovered.

ILLUSTRATION

The Bible says in Leviticus 17:11, *"For the life of the flesh is in the blood…."* This was not understood until very recent times. Even in the nineteenth century, doctors were using "blood letting" as a healing method. George Washington, America's first president, died from being a victim of this practice. Modern medicine has learned what the Bible has taught all along, that the life of the flesh is in the blood.

Though evidence is a strong proof for the Bible, it is important to understand that evidence alone is not our sole reason for believing that the Bible is indeed the Word of God. The Bible is our final authority regardless of the evidence.

QUOTE

"There's no better book with which to defend the Bible than the Bible itself."—**Dwight L. Moody**

Why should we read our Bible?

The Word of God brings growth.

As Christians, we must now read and study the Bible to learn how to take the next step of growth. First Peter 2:2 says, "*As newborn babes, desire the sincere milk of the word, that ye may grow thereby.*" Our attitude about God and His Word is so important, for it will determine the direction of our lives. We can know our Heavenly Father and His plans for our future by knowing His Word.

"*But grow in* _____, *and in the knowledge of our Lord and Saviour* _____ _____."—2 PETER 3:18A

The Word of God helps us resist temptation.

God has given His Word to man in order that it might show him how to live. The world is full of darkness, but the Word of God is a light that brightens our way.

"*Thy word is a* _____ *unto my feet, and a* _____ *unto my path.*"—PSALM 119:105

🔵 QUOTE

"This Bible will keep you from sin or sin will keep you from this Bible."—**Dwight L. Moody**

The Bible has power to change our lives.

The Bible has the power to change the lives of those who read and apply its truths. The most powerful external evidence of the Bible's claim to be the Word of God is the testimony of changed lives.

"For the word of God is quick, and _____, and sharper than any twoedged _____, piercing even to the dividing asunder of soul and spirit, and of the joints and marrow, and is a discerner of the _____ and intents of the heart."—Hebrews 4:12

💡 ILLUSTRATION

In 1876, while traveling together on a train, well-known atheists Robert Ingersoll and General Lew Wallace decided that Wallace should write a book dispelling the deity of Jesus and disproving the authenticity of the Bible. Wallace agreed, and immediately he began to immerse himself in the life of Christ.

As he poured over the pages of the Bible, he found "a conviction amounting to absolute belief in God and the divinity of Christ." Through his study, he concluded the Bible and Christ to be true, and became himself a devout Christian. General Wallace never wrote his book against the Bible. He wrote instead the classic Christian novel *Ben Hur: The Tale of the Christ.*

When should we read our Bible?

We should read our Bible daily.

The Bible is God's Word. This means it has authority over our lives. Because God is the author of the Bible, we must take His Word and apply its truths to all we say and do on a daily basis.

"…they received the word with all readiness of _____,

and searched the scriptures _____, whether those

*things were so."—*ACTS 17:11B

It is helpful to seek the Lord at the beginning of our day.

Because God's Word contains wisdom and practical truths for everyday living, it is important to begin each morning with time in His Word. Read the Bible and ask the Lord to help you apply His Word to the situations you will face that day.

"I love them that _____ me; and those that seek me

*_____ shall find me."—*PROVERBS 8:17

How should we read our Bible?

The Bible is a big book and can seem a little overwhelming at first. You do not have to read it cover to cover right away. Here are some ideas for beginning a Bible reading program.

The Gospels

New Christians could begin their Bible reading program by reading the first four books of the New Testament—Matthew, Mark, Luke, and John.

One-Year Bible Plan (included on page 89)

By reading four chapters a day, one can easily read through the entire Bible in a year.

A Proverb a Day

Proverbs is a good book to read as you begin your day, and it has thirty-one chapters—one chapter for each day of the month.

As you read each chapter, ask yourself the following questions:

1.   Is there a command here for me?
2.   Is there a sin I must forsake?
3.   Is there a promise I can claim?
4.   Is there some truth to gain?
5.   How is Christ revealed here?

Many Christians find it helpful to keep a Bible reading journal. This causes you to slow down and absorb God's Word. As you spend daily time with God, you can record Bible promises and important truths that God uses to speak to your heart. You may want to write down a prayer after you finish reading. Ask God to help you apply His Word to your life. You will find new meaning and spiritual renewal in recording and applying God's Word as you grow in spiritual maturity.

---

1.   Josh McDowell, *Evidence That Demands a Verdict* (San Bernardino: Here's Life Publishers, 1979), 17.
2.   Nelson Glueck, *Rivers in the Desert: A History of the Negev* (New York: Farrar, Strauss, and Cudahy, 1959), 31.
3.   William F. Albright, *Archaeology and the Religion of Israel* (Baltimore: John Hopkins, 1953), 176.
4.   Merrill Unger, *Unger's Bible Dictionary* (Chicago: Moody, 1971), 330.

CHAPTER EIGHT

LEARNING HOW TO PRAY

True Christianity is not just a set of beliefs, but a personal relationship with God. You come to know God by communicating with Him through prayer.

At first, you might feel awkward praying to someone you cannot even see, but as you continue talking to God, you will feel more comfortable. Remember that God loves you and enjoys hearing you pray. He has extended to you a way of communicating with Him at all times—day or night.

> *"Let us therefore come boldly unto the throne of grace, that we may obtain mercy, and find grace to help in time of need."*—HEBREWS 4:16

QUOTE

"Though a man shall have all knowledge about prayer, and though he understands all mysteries about prayer, unless he prays, he will never learn to pray."—**Chadwick, *The Path of Prayer***

« IMPORTANT TERMS

» **Mercy:** not getting what we deserve

» **Grace:** unearned favor

 « KEY BIBLE TRUTHS

Why do we pray?

Our Heavenly Father is interested in the small details of our lives.

God cares for each of the birds in the sky, although they are small and seemingly insignificant. Just imagine how much more He cares for even the smallest needs of each of His children!

"Behold the _____ of the air: for they sow not, neither do they reap, nor gather into barns; yet your _____ Father feedeth them. Are _____ not much _____ than they?"—MATTHEW 6:26

God hears us.

God promises to hear our requests. All we have to do to get His attention is ask!

"And this is the _____ that we have in him, that, if we _____ any thing according to his _____, he _____ us:"—1 JOHN 5:14

God cares about our troubles.

Sometimes our burdens can seem overwhelming, but God cares about our struggles and asks us to give them to Him.

"_____ all your _____ upon him; for he _____ for you."—1 PETER 5:7

God desires to grant our requests.

When we make a request to God, He always answers. Sometimes it may not be what we want to hear—He may say yes, no, or wait—but He always answers according to what is best for our lives.

"_____, and it shall be given you; _____, and ye shall find; knock, and it shall be _____unto you:"

—MATTHEW 7:7

How do we pray?

1. Have a quiet time. Choose a regular time every day when you can come away from your busy schedule and spend some quiet time with God.
2. Have a quiet place. Find a place that is free from distractions where you can pour out your heart to God.
3. Have a pure heart. Sin in your life can hinder your relationship with God. Ask the Lord to purify and cleanse your heart.
4. Have a sense of expectancy. Expect God to hear your prayers and answer your requests.
5. Have a list. Write down those things for which you want to pray and keep a record of when your prayers were answered.

What do we say? (You can easily remember by using the acrostic ACTS.)

ADORATION—giving the Lord the glory He deserves

God, our Creator, Saviour, and the King of kings, desires our worship and praise. We are to give Him glory, honor, and the respect He deserves.

"Give unto the LORD the _____ due unto his name;

_____ the LORD in the beauty of _____."

—PSALM 29:2

When the Lord Jesus taught His disciples how to pray, He began by teaching them to adore His Heavenly Father.

"And he said unto them, When ye pray, say, Our Father which art in heaven, _____ be thy name. Thy kingdom come. Thy will be done, as in heaven, so in earth."

—LUKE 11:2

CONFESSION—acknowledging and agreeing with God about our sin

Even though we are saved, we will often displease our Heavenly Father. We should regularly ask Him to forgive us and to cleanse the sins from our hearts.

"For I will _____ my iniquity; I will be _____ for my sin."—PSALM 38:18

THANKSGIVING—thanking the Lord for His goodness and blessings

God has done so much for us. He has given us eternal life, a home in Heaven, and an opportunity to serve Him. He has also blessed us with relationships and physical comfort here on earth. We should thank Him for His many blessings.

"*Enter into his gates with* _____, *and into his courts with* _____: *be thankful unto him, and* _____ *his name.*"—PSALM 100:4

SUPPLICATION—making specific requests to God

Throughout the New Testament, God promises to answer our prayers. He wants us to come before Him with our requests.

"*Be careful for nothing; but in every thing by* _____ *and supplication with thanksgiving let your* _____ *be made known unto God.*"—PHILIPPIANS 4:6

When should we pray?

We should pray daily.

"*Evening, and* _____, *and at noon, will I pray, and cry aloud: and he shall* _____ *my voice.*"—PSALM 55:17

We should pray at mealtimes.

"*(…they did eat* _____, *after that the Lord had given* _____:*)*"—JOHN 6:23B

We should pray all of the time.

"*Pray without* _____.*"*—1 THESSALONIANS 5:17

CHAPTER NINE

THE WITNESS OF A BELIEVER

God gave you the greatest gift—salvation, and He not only made this gift available to you, but to everyone in the world. After Christ rose, He left clear instructions for us to continue His mission of bringing hope to the world. Jesus said, *"...as my Father hath sent me, even so send I you"* (John 20:21). Just as someone took the time to show you how to get to Heaven, now God wants you to share the good news of eternal life with your friends and family.

Many Christians today are fearful of sharing the Gospel message. The truth is that the Gospel is clear and simple, and we can become comfortable sharing it with others. God promises that the Holy Spirit will guide and empower us as we share the good news of salvation. Acts 1:8 says, *"But ye shall receive power, after that the Holy Ghost is come upon you: and ye shall be witnesses unto me both in Jerusalem, and in all Judaea, and in Samaria, and unto the uttermost part of the earth."*

Someone once described evangelism as one beggar telling another beggar where he found bread. That is true. The message of the Gospel does not have to be complex. It should be so clear that even a child could understand.

 « IMPORTANT TERMS

» **Soulwinning:** personally sharing the good news of salvation with the lost

» **Witness:** a Christian who tells others about what Jesus Christ has done in his life

» **Gospel:** the good news that Christ died, was buried, and rose again the third day and has forgiven our sins

 « KEY BIBLE TRUTHS

We are to go and teach all nations about Jesus Christ.

Someone took time to share the good news of Jesus Christ with you. The Bible tells us that we are to tell others about salvation and eternity in Heaven.

"Go ye therefore, and _____ all nations, baptizing them in the name of the _____, and of the Son, and of the Holy Ghost: Teaching them to _____ all things whatsoever I have _____ you: and, lo, I am with you alway, even unto the end of the world. Amen."
—MATTHEW 28:19–20

We are to be fishers of men.

Very few things will last for eternity, but the souls of men will last forever, either in Heaven or in Hell. God wants us to spend our time "fishing" for the lost.

"And he (Jesus) saith unto them, _____ me, and I will make you _____ of men."—Matthew 4:19

We are entrusted with the Gospel.

God entrusted us with His Word for the purpose of seeing lost souls come to know Him. Are we going to use the Gospel for His glory?

"For our exhortation was not of _____, nor of uncleanness, nor in guile: But as we were allowed of God to be put in trust with the _____, even so we speak; not as pleasing men, but _____, which trieth our hearts."

—1 Thessalonians 2:3–4

Salvation is simple; it is something we can easily share with others. Commit the following truths to memory, and tell them to your family and friends today.

Three simple steps to sharing the Gospel with others:
1. We are all sinners.
    "For all have sinned, and come short of the glory of God;"—Romans 3:23

2. Christ died on the Cross because He loves us.
    "For God so loved the world, that he gave his only begotten Son, that whosoever believeth in him should not perish, but have everlasting life."—John 3:16

3. We may accept God's gift of eternal life by trusting in Him.

    "That if thou shalt confess with thy mouth the Lord Jesus, and shalt believe in thine heart that God hath raised him from the dead, thou shalt be saved."—ROMANS 10:9

 ILLUSTRATION

A little boy came home from school one day and announced to his parents that his Sunday school teacher was the grandmother of Jesus. "What makes you think that?" his dad asked. "Because," the young fellow replied, "she talks about Him all the time!"

A true love for Jesus will cause a Christian to be a wonderful witness for Christ.

CHAPTER TEN

BIBLE MEMORY

Some verses in the Bible will really touch your life. As a new believer, it is important to commit these verses to memory. Memorizing and meditating on Scripture will keep sin out of your life and will help you grow in your relationship with Jesus Christ.

Do not be discouraged as you begin memorizing verses from the Bible. As in all areas of life, memorization takes discipline and hard work. Your efforts will quickly pay off as God uses these verses to encourage and strengthen you every day.

QUOTE

"This book [the Bible] contains the mind of God, the state of man, the way of salvation, the doom of sinners and the happiness of believers. Its doctrines are holy, its precepts are binding, its histories are true, and its decisions are immutable. Read it to be wise, believe it to be safe and

practice it to be holy. It contains light to direct you, food to support you and comfort to cheer you. It is the traveller's map, the pilgrim's staff, the pilot's compass, the soldier's sword and the Christian's charter. Here paradise is restored, Heaven opened and the gates of Hell disclosed. Christ is its grand object, our good is its design and the glory of God its end. *It should fill the memory,* rule the heart, and guide the feet. Read it slowly, frequently, and prayerfully. It is a mine of wealth, a paradise of glory, and a river of pleasure. It is given you in life, will be opened in the judgement, and will be remembered forever. It involves the highest responsibility, will reward the greatest labour, and will condemn all who trifle with its sacred contents."
—Source Unknown

 « IMPORTANT TERMS

- » **Meditation:** thinking on God's Word and letting it work in our hearts
- » **Scripture Memorization:** memorizing specific verses from God's Word to help us avoid sin

 « KEY BIBLE TRUTHS

Why do we memorize the Bible?

We will experience good success in life.

The Bible gives us direction and advice for every area of our lives. If we really want to be successful in life and in the eyes of God, we must meditate on the Bible and apply its truths to our lives.

"This book of the law shall not _____ out of thy mouth; but thou shalt _____ therein day and night, that thou mayest _____ to do according to all that is written therein: for then thou shalt make thy way _____, and then thou shalt have good _____."—JOSHUA 1:8

We will avoid temptation and sin.

Our thoughts often determine our actions. When we think upon good things that please God, we can shut down the devil's temptation before a sin is ever committed.

"Thy _____ have I hid in mine _____, that I might not _____ against thee."—PSALM 119:11

How do we memorize the Bible?

Choose a specific time and place.

What gets scheduled gets accomplished. When memorizing the Word of God, you want to free yourself from all distractions.

Work out loud.

Even though it may sound odd, your mind memorizes better and faster that which it hears. Choose a specific time and quiet place for Scripture memorization and recitation.

Walk while you memorize.

Our bodies have a natural sense of rhythm. This is why we memorize the words of songs so quickly. We will memorize much more quickly (and retain it longer) if we are walking around.

Review, review, review.

Repetition is the key to learning. You cannot simply keep learning new passages weekly. You must make the time to review the previously memorized passages.

Set goals of time.

If you are not careful, you may ask for disappointment by setting goals of verses per week. The reason is that some verses are more difficult to learn than others. God will honor set goals of time spent in memorization.

QUOTE

"Sow a thought, reap an act. Sow an act, reap a habit. Sow a habit, reap a character. Sow a character, reap a destiny."
—E.D. Boardman

What verses do we memorize?

We have listed some important topics for the new Christian as well as several corresponding Bible verses. As you hide God's Word in your heart, you will gain new knowledge of the Bible and be able to share the Word of God with others.

The Bible
2 Timothy 3:16–17
Hebrews 4:12

God
John 4:24
Psalm 90:2

Jesus Christ
John 1:1, 14
Philippians 2:6–8
1 Timothy 3:16

Mankind
Genesis 1:26–27
Romans 3:10–11
Romans 3:23

Sin
Romans 6:23
James 1:15
1 John 1:8–10

Church
Colossians 1:18
Ephesians 5:25–27
Acts 2:46–47

Angels
Isaiah 6:1–3
Mark 13:32
Hebrews 1:5–6

End Times
John 14:1–3
Acts 1:10–11
Revelation 22:20

Salvation
John 14:6
Acts 4:12
Romans 10:9–10
Ephesians 2:8–9

CHAPTER ELEVEN

OVERCOMING SIN

B efore you were saved, you fulfilled the lusts of the flesh and the desires of your own heart. You were changed the day you received Christ, and you received a new nature at your salvation. Unfortunately, you will still face temptation. It is not a sin to be tempted. The Bible says that even Jesus was tempted—yet He was without sin (Hebrews 4:15). It is only when we succumb to the temptation that we commit sin.

When you sin, you do not lose your salvation, but your fellowship with the Lord may be broken, and you become a servant of sin. In order to avoid becoming a servant of sin, every Christian must reckon (account himself dead to sin and alive in Christ), and yield to what the Holy Spirit has to say.

> *"Likewise reckon ye also yourselves to be dead indeed unto sin, but alive unto God through Jesus Christ our Lord."*
> —ROMANS 6:11

"Know ye not, that to whom ye yield yourselves servants to obey, his servants ye are to whom ye obey; whether of sin unto death, or of obedience unto righteousness?"
—ROMANS 6:16

"I am crucified with Christ: nevertheless I live; yet not I, but Christ liveth in me: and the life which I now live in the flesh I live by the faith of the Son of God, who loved me, and gave himself for me."—GALATIANS 2:20

« IMPORTANT TERMS

» **Lust:** a desire for what is forbidden

» **Temptation:** that which moves us to sin

» **Flesh:** that which wars against our spirits

» **Sanctify:** to be set apart for God's use

« KEY BIBLE TRUTHS

What does the Bible say about overcoming sin?

I must hide God's Word in my heart.

Scripture memorization is so important. We can stop temptation before we act upon it by thinking and meditating on God's Word.

"Wherewithal shall a young man _____ his way? by taking heed thereto according to thy word. Thy _____ have I hid in mine _____, that I might not _____ against thee."—PSALM 119:9, 11

I must be sanctified by the truth of God's Word.

God's Word cleanses us and sets us apart for His use. It also strengthens us when we are tempted to sin.

"_____ them through thy _____: thy _____ is truth."—JOHN 17:17

I must confess and forsake my sins.

Even though we are saved, we will still do wrong. We can overcome our sin by continually asking God to forgive us for displeasing Him.

"He that covereth his _____ shall not prosper: but whoso _____ and _____ them shall have mercy."—PROVERBS 28:13

"If we _____ our sins, he is faithful and just to forgive us our sins, and to _____ us from all unrighteousness."—1 JOHN 1:9

I must be filled with the Spirit of God.

When we are filled with the Holy Spirit of God, we are less likely to act upon our temptations. The Holy Spirit provides a warning system or protection against sin.

"And be not drunk with wine, wherein is excess; but be _____ with the _____;"—EPHESIANS 5:18

ILLUSTRATION

A converted Indian once described to a missionary the battle between good and evil that went on within him. "I have two dogs living in me," he said, "a good dog and a mean dog. They are always fighting. The mean dog wants me to do bad things and the good dog wants me to do good things."

"Which dog wins?" asked the missionary.

"The one I feed the most!" replied the Indian.

It is the same in the Christian life. If you spend your time feeding your selfish desires, you will be too weak to fight temptation. It is only when we are filled with the Holy Spirit of God that we are less likely to act upon our temptations.

How do I overcome sin?

Do not allow sinful thoughts to linger.

When you think about sin, you are giving the devil room in your heart. When a sinful thought comes into your mind, immediately think on something that would please your Heavenly Father.

"_____ *down imaginations, and every* _____ *thing that exalteth itself against the knowledge of God, and bringing into* _____ *every thought to the obedience of Christ;*"—2 CORINTHIANS 10:5

Be aware of the traps of Satan.

Satan is your greatest enemy and will do everything in his power to cause you to displease Jesus Christ.

"Lest Satan should get an _____ *of us: for we are
not ignorant of his* _____*."*—2 CORINTHIANS 2:11

Satan's ultimate goal is to destroy you. He hates God and
wants to do anything he can to injure God's reputation.
Since he cannot touch God, he seeks to destroy God's glory
by attacking His children.

*"Be sober, be vigilant; because your adversary the devil, as a
roaring* _____*, walketh about, seeking whom
he may* _____*:"*—1 PETER 5:8

Do not associate with people or places
that make it easy for you to sin.

Those things that make it easy for you to do wrong should
be avoided. The old saying, "Nearness is likeness," is very
true. Begin to fill your life with relationships and activities
that would please God.

"But ____ *ye on the Lord Jesus Christ, and make not
provision for the* _____*, to fulfil the lusts thereof."*
—ROMANS 13:14

● QUOTE

"The thing that makes men and rivers crooked is following
the path of least resistance."—**Source Unknown**

Keep your life open and clean before God.

Ask the Lord to search your heart and show you those areas
in your life that displease Him.

"_____ me, O God, and know my heart: _____ me, and know my thoughts: And see if there be any wicked way in me, and _____ me in the way everlasting."

—PSALM 139:23–24

At times you might get a little discouraged because you battle the same temptations and sins over and over again. Don't get discouraged or lose hope. The Bible says in Philippians 1:6, *"Being confident of this very thing, that he which hath begun a good work in you will perform it until the day of Jesus Christ."*

CHAPTER TWELVE

BIBLICAL STEWARDSHIP

Everything we own belongs to God. We are simply stewards who manage God's possessions. The moment we accepted Christ, we became accountable for using wisely those things God has given us. Giving is an opportunity for us to invest in eternal riches, and it gets our eyes off the riches that fade away. All giving in the New Testament is done in and through the local church.

This world has a way of viewing money and material possessions. Those views are promoted through television, advertising, corporate and retail business, and a variety of other means. However, God's way of viewing money involves a simple concept called stewardship, and this view is presented to us in His Word.

« IMPORTANT TERMS

» **Tithing:** giving a portion (ten percent) of one's earnings to the local church in order to perform the Lord's work

» **Steward:** one who carefully oversees the possessions God has loaned him

» **Free-will Offering:** giving beyond the tithe as the Lord leads and instructs

« KEY BIBLE TRUTHS

The purpose of stewardship:

To Manage the Owner's Resources

Everything we have belongs to God. Though you may have worked hard to earn what you possess, it was God who gave you the sustenance to do what you did.

"But thou shalt remember the LORD thy God: for it is he that giveth thee power to get _____...."
—DEUTERONOMY 8:18

"The earth is the _____, and the fulness thereof; the world, and they that dwell therein."—PSALM 24:1

💬 **QUOTE**
"Owners have rights, stewards have responsibilities."
—**Source Unknown**

To Multiply the Owner's Resources

How do you *multiply* God's resources? One way is by making sound investments. Other ways would include not being wasteful or not becoming irresponsibly laden with debt. But one real way to get the best return out of your investment is to give it right back to God! Depositing the resources He has entrusted to you right back into His kingdom work is a sure way to multiply what He's given you. Because when those *temporal dollars* are invested into God's *eternal work*, they miraculously transform into eternally significant investments—especially when they help people hear and receive the Gospel of Jesus Christ (Matthew 25:14–29)!

"Not because I desire a gift: but I desire _____ that may abound to your account."—**PHILIPPIANS 4:17**

The Bible talks about several different kinds of stewardship:

The Tithe

A tithe is ten percent. As our love for the Lord grows, we willingly give ten percent of our income to Him. It is amazing how the Lord blesses this simple act of obedience. Many Christians have seen God give them more than they ever had before they started tithing.

"And here men that die receive _____; but there he receiveth them, of whom it is witnessed that he _____."

—**HEBREWS 7:8**

"Bring ye all the _____ into the storehouse, that there may be meat in mine house, and _____ me now herewith, saith the LORD of hosts, if I will not open you the windows of heaven, and pour you out a _____, that there shall not be room enough to receive it."

—MALACHI 3:10

Cheerful Giving

As we grow in the Lord, we cheerfully give beyond ten percent because we understand God blesses giving.

"Every man according as he _____ in his heart, so let him _____; not grudgingly, or of necessity: for God loveth a _____ giver."—2 CORINTHIANS 9:7

As God prospers us for keeping Him first in our lives, we give back to Him according to the amount of His blessings.

"Upon the first day of the week let _____ one of you lay by him in store, as _____ hath _____ him, that there be no gatherings when I come."—1 CORINTHIANS 16:2

As you begin biblical giving, you will quickly learn the joys that come from giving to the Lord. You will learn how God meets all of your needs, even when your finances do not work out on paper. You will enjoy hearing the reports of those saved on the mission field as a result of your financial help.

"For where your treasure is, there will your heart be also."—LUKE 12:34

CHAPTER THIRTEEN

WHAT IS A BAPTIST?

The word *Baptist* was first used in English literature in 1644. The name was not chosen by themselves but by their opponents. They were commonly called Anabaptists because they refused to baptize infants. Over time, the term *Anabaptist* fell out of vogue, and the name *Baptist* became the popular term of use.

Baptists are not Protestants. Baptists did not come *out* of the Reformation Movement, they came *through* it. Those denominations who trace their roots to the Reformation are considered Protestant because they were a part of the "Protest" movement against the Roman Catholic institution as members. Baptists were never *out of* nor a *part of* the Roman Catholic religion.

Baptist churches have eight primary teachings from the Bible that set them apart from other churches or denominations. These teachings are listed on the following pages in the acrostic, BAPTISTS.

« IMPORTANT TERMS

» **Ordinance:** a biblical practice exercised in the local church

» **The Lord's Table:** symbolizes Christ's death, burial, and resurrection and is a time of remembrance for believers

» **Office:** a position of authority within the church

 « KEY BIBLE TRUTHS

B—Bible authority in all matters of faith and practice

The church does not exercise visions, revelations, tongues, or extra biblical "messages from God." We uphold the truths of the Bible as our supreme authority in the church. (Acts 17:11; 2 Timothy 3:16–17; Hebrews 4:12; 2 Peter 1:21)

"Sanctify them through thy _____: thy _____ is truth."—JOHN 17:17

A—Autonomy or self-governing power of the local church

We are completely independent from other churches, boards, or denominations. Christ is the head of our church. (1 Timothy 3:15; Acts 20:19–30)

"And he [Jesus] is the_____ of the body, the _____: who is the beginning, the firstborn from the dead; that in ____ things he might have the _____."

—COLOSSIANS 1:18

P—Priesthood (direct access to God) of each believer

Every believer has equal and instant access to God. This means that each believer is his own priest and has direct access to God's truth and God's will for his life.

"Seeing then that we have a great _____ _____,

that is passed into the heavens, _____ the Son of God,

let us hold fast our profession. For we have not an high priest

which cannot be touched with the feeling of our infirmities;

but was in all points tempted like as we are, yet without _____.

Let us therefore come _____ unto the throne of _____

, that we may obtain mercy, and find _____ to help in

time of need."—HEBREWS 4:14–16

"Ye also, as lively stones, are built up a spiritual house, an holy

_____, to offer up spiritual sacrifices,

acceptable to God by Jesus Christ."—1 PETER 2:5

T—Two offices within the church

The church has two offices of leadership—pastors and deacons. Scripture refers to the office of pastor with terms such as elder, bishop, and pastor. It is the responsibility of the pastor to serve the church by leading, teaching, and overseeing the church work. It is the responsibility of the deacons to serve the church family through assisting with care and the provision of special needs. (Acts 6:1–7; 1 Timothy 3:1–13; Titus 1:6–9; 1 Peter 5:1–4)

I—Individual soul liberty

Every man and woman must choose personally to come to Christ for salvation. No one (including pastors, priests, etc.) can intervene or make the decision for them. (Romans 14:1–8, 12–23)

"So then _____ *cometh by* _____ *, and hearing by the* _____ *of God."*—ROMANS 10:17

S—Separation of church and state

The state should have no power to intervene in the free expression of religious liberty. (Acts 5:29–31; Romans 13:1–4)

"…Render therefore unto _____ *the things which are Caesar's; and unto* _____ *the things that are God's."*

—MATTHEW 22:21B

T—Two ordinances

The church practices two simple ordinances—baptism and the Lord's Table (communion). These ordinances have no part in salvation and only serve as pictures of what Christ did for us on the Cross. (Matthew 28:18–20; Acts 2:38–43; Acts 8:36–38; Romans 6:1–6; 1 Corinthians 11:23–24)

S—Saved membership only

We do not place infants on our membership list. Each member, regardless of age, must give a testimony of salvation (a conversion experience).

CONCLUSION

Congratulations! You have just completed *First Steps for New Christians*, and your new life in Christ is off to a great start! It is now time to take the next step in Christian growth by following the Lord in believer's baptism and by becoming a part of a local, Bible-believing church. Do not hesitate to take this next step—there is nothing to fear in obeying Christ. You will discover a new level of support from a caring pastor and experience unbelievable joy in becoming involved in a loving church family.

You may have been given this booklet at church. Plan to attend the next service and take the opportunity to speak to the pastor or another member. They will be happy to help you continue your Christian growth. Maybe you received this booklet from the person who led you to the Lord. Talk to that person if you are unsure of how to find a Bible-believing church. You may also access our ministry online at strivingtogether.com. We have many resources available that will assist and encourage your new walk with God.

First Steps for New Christians provided you with basic information and insight to help you grow into an abundant relationship with Jesus Christ. Remember this is only the commencement—the beginning of a future filled with hope as you experience more deeply the joy of knowing God and His plan for your life.

Sincerely,

Paul Chappell

Pastor Paul Chappell

one year
BIBLE READING
schedule

January

- ☐ **1** Gen. 1–3   Matt. 1
- ☐ **2** Gen. 4–6   Matt. 2
- ☐ **3** Gen. 7–9   Matt. 3
- ☐ **4** Gen. 10–12   Matt. 4
- ☐ **5** Gen. 13–15   Matt. 5:1–26
- ☐ **6** Gen. 16–17   Matt. 5:27–48
- ☐ **7** Gen. 18–19   Matt. 6:1–18
- ☐ **8** Gen. 20–22   Matt. 6:19–34
- ☐ **9** Gen. 23–24   Matt. 7
- ☐ **10** Gen. 25–26   Matt. 8:1–17
- ☐ **11** Gen. 27–28   Matt. 8:18–34
- ☐ **12** Gen. 29–30   Matt. 9:1–17
- ☐ **13** Gen. 31–32   Matt. 9:18–38
- ☐ **14** Gen. 33–35   Matt. 10:1–20
- ☐ **15** Gen. 36–38   Matt. 10:21–42
- ☐ **16** Gen. 39–40   Matt. 11
- ☐ **17** Gen. 41–42   Matt. 12:1–23
- ☐ **18** Gen. 43–45   Matt. 12:24–50
- ☐ **19** Gen. 46–48   Matt. 13:1–30
- ☐ **20** Gen. 49–50   Matt. 13:31–58
- ☐ **21** Ex. 1–3   Matt. 14:1–21
- ☐ **22** Ex. 4–6   Matt. 14:22–36
- ☐ **23** Ex. 7–8   Matt. 15:1–20
- ☐ **24** Ex. 9–11   Matt. 15:21–39
- ☐ **25** Ex. 12–13   Matt. 16
- ☐ **26** Ex. 14–15   Matt. 17
- ☐ **27** Ex. 16–18   Matt. 18:1–20
- ☐ **28** Ex. 19–20   Matt. 18:21–35
- ☐ **29** Ex. 21–22   Matt. 19
- ☐ **30** Ex. 23–24   Matt. 20:1–16
- ☐ **31** Ex. 25–26   Matt. 20:17–34

February

- ☐ **1** Ex. 27–28   Matt. 21:1–22
- ☐ **2** Ex. 29–30   Matt. 21:23–46
- ☐ **3** Ex. 31–33   Matt. 22:1–22
- ☐ **4** Ex. 34–35   Matt. 22:23–46
- ☐ **5** Ex. 36–38   Matt. 23:1–22
- ☐ **6** Ex. 39–40   Matt. 23:23–39
- ☐ **7** Lev. 1–3   Matt. 24:1–28
- ☐ **8** Lev. 4–5   Matt. 24:29–51
- ☐ **9** Lev. 6–7   Matt. 25:1–30
- ☐ **10** Lev. 8–10   Matt. 25:31–46
- ☐ **11** Lev. 11–12   Matt. 26:1–25
- ☐ **12** Lev. 13   Matt. 26:26–50
- ☐ **13** Lev. 14   Matt. 26:51–75
- ☐ **14** Lev. 15–16   Matt. 27:1–26
- ☐ **15** Lev. 17–18   Matt. 27:27–50
- ☐ **16** Lev. 19–20   Matt. 27:51–66
- ☐ **17** Lev. 21–22   Matt. 28
- ☐ **18** Lev. 23–24   Mark 1:1–22
- ☐ **19** Lev. 25   Mark 1:23–45
- ☐ **20** Lev. 26–27   Mark 2
- ☐ **21** Num. 1–2   Mark 3:1–19
- ☐ **22** Num. 3–4   Mark 3:20–35
- ☐ **23** Num. 5–6   Mark 4:1–20
- ☐ **24** Num. 7–8   Mark 4:21–41
- ☐ **25** Num. 9–11   Mark 5:1–20
- ☐ **26** Num. 12–14   Mark 5:21–43
- ☐ **27** Num. 15–16   Mark 6:1–29
- ☐ **28** Num. 17–19   Mark 6:30–56

March

☐	1	Num. 20–22	Mark 7:1–13
☐	2	Num. 23–25	Mark 7:14–37
☐	3	Num. 26–28	Mark 8
☐	4	Num. 29–31	Mark 9:1–29
☐	5	Num. 32–34	Mark 9:30–50
☐	6	Num. 35–36	Mark 10:1–31
☐	7	Deut. 1–3	Mark 10:32–52
☐	8	Deut. 4–6	Mark 11:1–18
☐	9	Deut. 7–9	Mark 11:19–33
☐	10	Deut. 10–12	Mark 12:1–27
☐	11	Deut. 13–15	Mark 12:28–44
☐	12	Deut. 16–18	Mark 13:1–20
☐	13	Deut. 19–21	Mark 13:21–37
☐	14	Deut. 22–24	Mark 14:1–26
☐	15	Deut. 25–27	Mark 14:27–53
☐	16	Deut. 28–29	Mark 14:54–72
☐	17	Deut. 30–31	Mark 15:1–25
☐	18	Deut. 32–34	Mark 15:26–47
☐	19	Josh. 1–3	Mark 16
☐	20	Josh. 4–6	Luke 1:1–20
☐	21	Josh. 7–9	Luke 1:21–38
☐	22	Josh. 10–12	Luke 1:39–56
☐	23	Josh. 13–15	Luke 1:57–80
☐	24	Josh. 16–18	Luke 2:1–24
☐	25	Josh. 19–21	Luke 2:25–52
☐	26	Josh. 22–24	Luke 3
☐	27	Judges 1–3	Luke 4:1–30
☐	28	Judges 4–6	Luke 4:31–44
☐	29	Judges 7–8	Luke 5:1–16
☐	30	Judges 9–10	Luke 5:17–39
☐	31	Judges 11–12	Luke 6:1–26

April

☐	1	Judges 13–15	Luke 6:27–49
☐	2	Judges 16–18	Luke 7:1–30
☐	3	Judges 19–21	Luke 7:31–50
☐	4	Ruth 1–4	Luke 8:1–25
☐	5	1 Sam. 1–3	Luke 8:26–56
☐	6	1 Sam. 4–6	Luke 9:1–17
☐	7	1 Sam. 7–9	Luke 9:18–36
☐	8	1 Sam. 10–12	Luke 9:37–62
☐	9	1 Sam. 13–14	Luke 10:1–24
☐	10	1 Sam. 15–16	Luke 10:25–42
☐	11	1 Sam. 17–18	Luke 11:1–28
☐	12	1 Sam. 19–21	Luke 11:29–54
☐	13	1 Sam. 22–24	Luke 12:1–31
☐	14	1 Sam. 25–26	Luke 12:32–59
☐	15	1 Sam. 27–29	Luke 13:1–22
☐	16	1 Sam. 30–31	Luke 13:23–35
☐	17	2 Sam. 1–2	Luke 14:1–24
☐	18	2 Sam. 3–5	Luke 14:25–35
☐	19	2 Sam. 6–8	Luke 15:1–10
☐	20	2 Sam. 9–11	Luke 15:11–32
☐	21	2 Sam. 12–13	Luke 16
☐	22	2 Sam. 14–15	Luke 17:1–19
☐	23	2 Sam. 16–18	Luke 17:20–37
☐	24	2 Sam. 19–20	Luke 18:1–23
☐	25	2 Sam. 21–22	Luke 18:24–43
☐	26	2 Sam. 23–24	Luke 19:1–27
☐	27	1 Kings 1–2	Luke 19:28–48
☐	28	1 Kings 3–5	Luke 20:1–26
☐	29	1 Kings 6–7	Luke 20:27–47
☐	30	1 Kings 8–9	Luke 21:1–19

May

☐	1	1 Kings 10–11	Luke 21:20–38
☐	2	1 Kings 12–13	Luke 22:1–30
☐	3	1 Kings 14–15	Luke 22:31–46
☐	4	1 Kings 16–18	Luke 22:47–71
☐	5	1 Kings 19–20	Luke 23:1–25
☐	6	1 Kings 21–22	Luke 23:26–56
☐	7	2 Kings 1–3	Luke 24:1–35
☐	8	2 Kings 4–6	Luke 24:36–53
☐	9	2 Kings 7–9	John 1:1–28
☐	10	2 Kings 10–12	John 1:29–51
☐	11	2 Kings 13–14	John 2
☐	12	2 Kings 15–16	John 3:1–18
☐	13	2 Kings 17–18	John 3:19–36
☐	14	2 Kings 19–21	John 4:1–30
☐	15	2 Kings 22–23	John 4:31–54
☐	16	2 Kings 24–25	John 5:1–24
☐	17	1 Chr. 1–3	John 5:25–47
☐	18	1 Chr. 4–6	John 6:1–21
☐	19	1 Chr. 7–9	John 6:22–44
☐	20	1 Chr. 10–12	John 6:45–71
☐	21	1 Chr. 13–15	John 7:1–27
☐	22	1 Chr. 16–18	John 7:28–53
☐	23	1 Chr. 19–21	John 8:1–27
☐	24	1 Chr. 22–24	John 8:28–59
☐	25	1 Chr. 25–27	John 9:1–23
☐	26	1 Chr. 28–29	John 9:24–41
☐	27	2 Chr. 1–3	John 10:1–23
☐	28	2 Chr. 4–6	John 10:24–42
☐	29	2 Chr. 7–9	John 11:1–29
☐	30	2 Chr. 10–12	John 11:30–57
☐	31	2 Chr. 13–14	John 12:1–26

June

☐	1	2 Chr. 15–16	John 12:27–50
☐	2	2 Chr. 17–18	John 13:1–20
☐	3	2 Chr. 19–20	John 13:21–38
☐	4	2 Chr. 21–22	John 14
☐	5	2 Chr. 23–24	John 15
☐	6	2 Chr. 25–27	John 16
☐	7	2 Chr. 28–29	John 17
☐	8	2 Chr. 30–31	John 18:1–18
☐	9	2 Chr. 32–33	John 18:19–40
☐	10	2 Chr. 34–36	John 19:1–22
☐	11	Ezra 1–2	John 19:23–42
☐	12	Ezra 3–5	John 20
☐	13	Ezra 6–8	John 21
☐	14	Ezra 9–10	Acts 1
☐	15	Neh. 1–3	Acts 2:1–21
☐	16	Neh. 4–6	Acts 2:22–47
☐	17	Neh. 7–9	Acts 3
☐	18	Neh. 10–11	Acts 4:1–22
☐	19	Neh. 12–13	Acts 4:23–37
☐	20	Esther 1–2	Acts 5:1–21
☐	21	Esther 3–5	Acts 5:22–42
☐	22	Esther 6–8	Acts 6
☐	23	Esther 9–10	Acts 7:1–21
☐	24	Job 1–2	Acts 7:22–43
☐	25	Job 3–4	Acts 7:44–60
☐	26	Job 5–7	Acts 8:1–25
☐	27	Job 8–10	Acts 8:26–40
☐	28	Job 11–13	Acts 9:1–21
☐	29	Job 14–16	Acts 9:22–43
☐	30	Job 17–19	Acts 10:1–23

July

☐	1	Job 20–21	Acts 10:24–48
☐	2	Job 22–24	Acts 11
☐	3	Job 25–27	Acts 12
☐	4	Job 28–29	Acts 13:1–25
☐	5	Job 30–31	Acts 13:26–52
☐	6	Job 32–33	Acts 14
☐	7	Job 34–35	Acts 15:1–21
☐	8	Job 36–37	Acts 15:22–41
☐	9	Job 38–40	Acts 16:1–21
☐	10	Job 41–42	Acts 16:22–40
☐	11	Ps. 1–3	Acts 17:1–15
☐	12	Ps. 4–6	Acts 17:16–34
☐	13	Ps. 7–9	Acts 18
☐	14	Ps. 10–12	Acts 19:1–20
☐	15	Ps. 13–15	Acts 19:21–41
☐	16	Ps. 16–17	Acts 20:1–16
☐	17	Ps. 18–19	Acts 20:17–38
☐	18	Ps. 20–22	Acts 21:1–17
☐	19	Ps. 23–25	Acts 21:18–40
☐	20	Ps. 26–28	Acts 22
☐	21	Ps. 29–30	Acts 23:1–15
☐	22	Ps. 31–32	Acts 23:16–35
☐	23	Ps. 33–34	Acts 24
☐	24	Ps. 35–36	Acts 25
☐	25	Ps. 37–39	Acts 26
☐	26	Ps. 40–42	Acts 27:1–26
☐	27	Ps. 43–45	Acts 27:27–44
☐	28	Ps. 46–48	Acts 28
☐	29	Ps. 49–50	Rom. 1
☐	30	Ps. 51–53	Rom. 2
☐	31	Ps. 54–56	Rom. 3

August

☐	1	Ps. 57–59	Rom. 4
☐	2	Ps. 60–62	Rom. 5
☐	3	Ps. 63–65	Rom. 6
☐	4	Ps. 66–67	Rom. 7
☐	5	Ps. 68–69	Rom. 8:1–21
☐	6	Ps. 70–71	Rom. 8:22–39
☐	7	Ps. 72–73	Rom. 9:1–15
☐	8	Ps. 74–76	Rom. 9:16–33
☐	9	Ps. 77–78	Rom. 10
☐	10	Ps. 79–80	Rom. 11:1–18
☐	11	Ps. 81–83	Rom. 11:19–36
☐	12	Ps. 84–86	Rom. 12
☐	13	Ps. 87–88	Rom. 13
☐	14	Ps. 89–90	Rom. 14
☐	15	Ps. 91–93	Rom. 15:1–13
☐	16	Ps. 94–96	Rom. 15:14–33
☐	17	Ps. 97–99	Rom. 16
☐	18	Ps. 100–102	1 Cor. 1
☐	19	Ps. 103–104	1 Cor. 2
☐	20	Ps. 105–106	1 Cor. 3
☐	21	Ps. 107–109	1 Cor. 4
☐	22	Ps. 110–112	1 Cor. 5
☐	23	Ps. 113–115	1 Cor. 6
☐	24	Ps. 116–118	1 Cor. 7:1–19
☐	25	Ps. 119:1–88	1 Cor. 7:20–40
☐	26	Ps. 119:89–176	1 Cor. 8
☐	27	Ps. 120–122	1 Cor. 9
☐	28	Ps.123–125	1 Cor. 10:1–18
☐	29	Ps. 126–128	1 Cor. 10:19–33
☐	30	Ps. 129–131	1 Cor. 11:1–16
☐	31	Ps. 132–134	1 Cor. 11:17–34

September

☐	1	Ps. 135–136	1 Cor. 12
☐	2	Ps. 137–139	1 Cor. 13
☐	3	Ps. 140–142	1 Cor. 14:1–20
☐	4	Ps. 143–145	1 Cor. 14:21–40
☐	5	Ps. 146–147	1 Cor. 15:1–28
☐	6	Ps. 148–150	1 Cor. 15:29–58
☐	7	Prov. 1–2	1 Cor. 16
☐	8	Prov. 3–5	2 Cor. 1
☐	9	Prov. 6–7	2 Cor. 2
☐	10	Prov. 8–9	2 Cor. 3
☐	11	Prov. 10–12	2 Cor. 4
☐	12	Prov. 13–15	2 Cor. 5
☐	13	Prov. 16–18	2 Cor. 6
☐	14	Prov. 19–21	2 Cor. 7
☐	15	Prov. 22–24	2 Cor. 8
☐	16	Prov. 25–26	2 Cor. 9
☐	17	Prov. 27–29	2 Cor. 10
☐	18	Prov. 30–31	2 Cor. 11:1–15
☐	19	Eccl. 1–3	2 Cor. 11:16–33
☐	20	Eccl. 4–6	2 Cor. 12
☐	21	Eccl. 7–9	2 Cor. 13
☐	22	Eccl. 10–12	Gal. 1
☐	23	Song 1–3	Gal. 2
☐	24	Song 4–5	Gal. 3
☐	25	Song 6–8	Gal. 4
☐	26	Isa. 1–2	Gal. 5
☐	27	Isa. 3–4	Gal. 6
☐	28	Isa. 5–6	Eph. 1
☐	29	Isa. 7–8	Eph. 2
☐	30	Isa. 9–10	Eph. 3

October

☐	1	Isa. 11–13	Eph. 4
☐	2	Isa. 14–16	Eph. 5:1–16
☐	3	Isa. 17–19	Eph. 5:17–33
☐	4	Isa. 20–22	Eph. 6
☐	5	Isa. 23–25	Phil. 1
☐	6	Isa. 26–27	Phil. 2
☐	7	Isa. 28–29	Phil. 3
☐	8	Isa. 30–31	Phil. 4
☐	9	Isa. 32–33	Col. 1
☐	10	Isa. 34–36	Col. 2
☐	11	Isa. 37–38	Col. 3
☐	12	Isa. 39–40	Col. 4
☐	13	Isa. 41–42	1 Thess. 1
☐	14	Isa. 43–44	1 Thess. 2
☐	15	Isa. 45–46	1 Thess. 3
☐	16	Isa. 47–49	1 Thess. 4
☐	17	Isa. 50–52	1 Thess. 5
☐	18	Isa. 53–55	2 Thess. 1
☐	19	Isa. 56–58	2 Thess. 2
☐	20	Isa. 59–61	2 Thess. 3
☐	21	Isa. 62–64	1 Tim. 1
☐	22	Isa. 65–66	1 Tim. 2
☐	23	Jer. 1–2	1 Tim. 3
☐	24	Jer. 3–5	1 Tim. 4
☐	25	Jer. 6–8	1 Tim. 5
☐	26	Jer. 9–11	1 Tim. 6
☐	27	Jer. 12–14	2 Tim. 1
☐	28	Jer. 15–17	2 Tim. 2
☐	29	Jer. 18–19	2 Tim. 3
☐	30	Jer. 20–21	2 Tim. 4
☐	31	Jer. 22–23	Titus 1

November

☐	**1**	Jer. 24–26	Titus 2
☐	**2**	Jer. 27–29	Titus 3
☐	**3**	Jer. 30–31	Philemon
☐	**4**	Jer. 32–33	Heb. 1
☐	**5**	Jer. 34–36	Heb. 2
☐	**6**	Jer. 37–39	Heb. 3
☐	**7**	Jer. 40–42	Heb. 4
☐	**8**	Jer. 43–45	Heb. 5
☐	**9**	Jer. 46–47	Heb. 6
☐	**10**	Jer. 48–49	Heb. 7
☐	**11**	Jer. 50	Heb. 8
☐	**12**	Jer. 51–52	Heb. 9
☐	**13**	Lam. 1–2	Heb. 10:1–18
☐	**14**	Lam. 3–5	Heb. 10:19–39
☐	**15**	Ezek. 1–2	Heb. 11:1–19
☐	**16**	Ezek. 3–4	Heb. 11:20–40
☐	**17**	Ezek. 5–7	Heb. 12
☐	**18**	Ezek. 8–10	Heb. 13
☐	**19**	Ezek. 11–13	James 1
☐	**20**	Ezek. 14–15	James 2
☐	**21**	Ezek. 16–17	James 3
☐	**22**	Ezek. 18–19	James 4
☐	**23**	Ezek. 20–21	James 5
☐	**24**	Ezek. 22–23	1 Peter 1
☐	**25**	Ezek. 24–26	1 Peter 2
☐	**26**	Ezek. 27–29	1 Peter 3
☐	**27**	Ezek. 30–32	1 Peter 4
☐	**28**	Ezek. 33–34	1 Peter 5
☐	**29**	Ezek. 35–36	2 Peter 1
☐	**30**	Ezek. 37–39	2 Peter 2

December

☐	**1**	Ezek. 40–41	2 Peter 3
☐	**2**	Ezek. 42–44	1 John 1
☐	**3**	Ezek. 45–46	1 John 2
☐	**4**	Ezek. 47–48	1 John 3
☐	**5**	Dan. 1–2	1 John 4
☐	**6**	Dan. 3–4	1 John 5
☐	**7**	Dan. 5–7	2 John
☐	**8**	Dan. 8–10	3 John
☐	**9**	Dan. 11–12	Jude
☐	**10**	Hos. 1–4	Rev. 1
☐	**11**	Hos. 5–8	Rev. 2
☐	**12**	Hos. 9–11	Rev. 3
☐	**13**	Hos. 12–14	Rev. 4
☐	**14**	Joel	Rev. 5
☐	**15**	Amos 1–3	Rev. 6
☐	**16**	Amos 4–6	Rev. 7
☐	**17**	Amos 7–9	Rev. 8
☐	**18**	Obad.	Rev. 9
☐	**19**	Jonah	Rev. 10
☐	**20**	Micah 1–3	Rev. 11
☐	**21**	Micah 4–5	Rev. 12
☐	**22**	Micah 6–7	Rev. 13
☐	**23**	Nahum	Rev. 14
☐	**24**	Hab.	Rev. 15
☐	**25**	Zeph.	Rev. 16
☐	**26**	Hag.	Rev. 17
☐	**27**	Zech. 1–4	Rev. 18
☐	**28**	Zech. 5–8	Rev. 19
☐	**29**	Zech. 9–12	Rev. 20
☐	**30**	Zech. 13–14	Rev. 21
☐	**31**	Mal.	Rev. 22

DAILY IN THE WORD

Visit **dailyintheword.org** to receive
- daily devotionals from Dr. Paul Chappell
- daily radio broadcasts
- helps from the Scriptures

STRIVING TOGETHER

Visit **strivingtogether.com** to find
- helpful Christian books
- Christ-honoring music
- resources for Christian growth

Striving Together
PUBLICATIONS

4020 E. Lancaster Blvd.
Lancaster, CA 93535
800.201.7748
strivingtogether.com